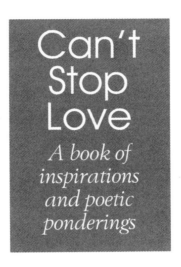

Can't Stop Love

A book of inspirations and poetic ponderings

Sherri D. Dyson

SDD *Publications*
Sarasota, Florida

Can't Stop Love by Sherri D. Dyson
Published by SDD Publications
Sherri D. Dyson
2335 University Parkway
Sarasota, Florida
email: Sherridd@aol.com
website: SDDministries.org

Unless otherwise noted, all Scripture quotations are from the King James Version of the Bible.

Scripture taken from the HOLY BIBLE, NEW INTERNATIONAL VERSION ® Copyright © 1973, 1978, 1984 by International Bible Society. Used by permission of Zondervan Publishing House. All rights reserved.

The "NIV" and "New International Version" trademarks are registered in the United States Patent and Trademark Office by International Bible Society. Use of either trademark requires the permission of International Bible Society.

Library of Congress Cataloging-in-Publication Data
Dyson, Sherri D. (Sherri Denise)
Can't Stop Love / Sherri D. Dyson

Edited by Joanne Derstine
Graphic Design by Jeff Johnson
Typesetting by Connie Zimmermann, Joanne Derstine &
Kevin Washington

Printed by Faith Printing Co., Taylors, SC

CONTENTS

Dedication 6

Acknowledgments 7

Author's Pen 8

Foreword 10

Introduction 11

PART 1 - Love
    Lifetime Commitment 15
    Can't Stop Love 18
    Language Of Love 19
    Love Of My Life 20
    Perfect Fit 21
    Make Believe World 22
    One Of A Kind 23
    Discovering You Discovering Me 24
    Together In The Heart 25

PART 2 - Children
    Heirloom Memories 29
    Innocence 31

PART 3 - Wedding
    Uniquely Wed 35
    Faithfully 37
    More Than A Promise 38
    Song Of Love 39
    Destiny 40

PART 4 - Last Good-bye
    Hand Crocheted Booties 43
    Love Stories 4/
    Love's Legacy ....

PART 5 - Spiritual

S.T.O.P. - See The Overall Picture 49

His Purpose In Me 51

The Battlefield Of My Mind 52

Questions And Answers 54

Stop The Insanity 55

Face In A Crowd 57

Eyes Unseen 58

My Favorite Place 59

Praise Anyway 60

Please Understand 61

From Emptiness To Fullness 62

The One My Heart Loves 63

By My Side 64

Images 65

Giving Away My Pain 67

Godly Thoughts 68

PART 6 - Seasonal

Springtime Flower Frostbitten By Winter Chill 71

Special Delivery 75

Seasons Of Life 77

Creating World 78

Moon's Eye 79

PART 7 - Animal Lovers

Nine Lives Times Three 83

Curious Creatures 86

PART 8 - Mother's Day

In The Form Of A Woman 91

Woman To Woman 94

My Mother, My Friend 95

The One Who Dreamed Of Me 97

Silent Applaud 98

A Lady 99

PART 9 - Father's Day

Prayer Cries Help 103

Prayer Cries Help (poem) 105

Uniquely True 106

It's Me 107

Time Flies 108

PART 10 - Christmas

Unwrap Your Gifts 113

Let Us Not Forget 116

PART 11 - New Years

365 Cockcrows 119

A New Heart 121

Temporary Solutions 122

Afterthoughts 123

Caption Quotes 125

In Black And White 127

DEDICATION

I choose to devote this book to the man who inspired the title poem, *Can't Stop Love*. His enthusiasm for life has given me a shot in the arm to awaken a sleeping verse maker from a 32-year slumber. While his charmed countenance speaks volumes to my soul, his animated gestures breathe life into my sense of humor, and his anointed exhortation provokes my spirit to energy.

He has touched-up the picture of my life with the perfected brush of friendship, love, marriage, the gift of his two sons, Adrian and Aaron, and our miracle baby boy, Preston Kendall.

I know him as friend, husband, pastor, pilot, and Timothy J. Dyson. But more than that, I know him as the love of my life.

There is no fear in love; but perfect love casteth out fear: because fear hath torment. He that feareth is not made perfect in love. (I John 4:18).

ACKNOWLEDGMENTS

Many individuals have made significant contributions of laughter and love into my vital spirit, but only a handful have allowed me to collect interest on the immense deposit recorded in my daily journal.

The two that conceived one named Sherri D., nurtured me through infancy, functioned as my number one coach during adolescence, befriended me as a young adult, and continue to promote my endeavors are Rev. and Mrs. Richard W. Motes, Sr., my parents.

Dad and Mom, thank you for prompting me as a little girl to run toward God. In pursuit of Him, I unearthed the proficiency of a poet.

Enthusiasm administered by Connie Zimmermann played an essential role in developing *Can't Stop Love*.

Connie, you are one of a kind. Thank you for organizing my thoughts and polishing my inspirations.

The finished product, perfected by Joanne Derstine, reflects professionalism at its peak. Her patience was tried and proven to be true.

Joanne, thank you for taking an amateur and developing an author.

The God of all gods, creator of artists, poet in motion, and giver of life whispered words of rhyme and reason into my listening ears, inducing *Can't Stop Love*. When it came to accomplishing my dream of fiction, He left no stoned unturned to substantiate a figment of my imagination into a fact of life. That is my God!

Heavenly Father, thank you for confiding in me.

AUTHOR'S PEN

Dear Reader:

My episode called *Life* aires a series of events recycled by word of mouth rhythmical compositions. As author of poetry, songs, psalms, and inspirations, I put pen to paper to audition before my constructive critic, the producer of *Life*. With two thumbs up, He indicates by heart how to represent *Life* to spectators in hot pursuit of thought-provoking and entertaining lines. By stimulating brain waves through rhythm and rhyme of mere words, my piece is pronounced a take, only when emotions stir boughs of laughter and trigger rivers of tears.

Life premiered in a glass house next door to the house of prayer. The community of worshipers mimicked Siskel and Ebert, compelling ratings to sky-rocket or nose-dive, contingent upon public display of the preacher's kid.

As one might expect, my grown-up role sheds light upon the wife of a Pastor. By staying in character, recurrent storylines instruct me to weather the storm and celebrate the rainbow.

Passion and pain gained from my position in *Life* has chartered a course down a road less traveled. In any event, *Life's* season finale will be determined by how well I follow directions.

My ultimate goal in reenacting my signature show of *Life* upon the pages of *Can't Stop Love* is to give rise to happy memories and future victories within the heart of you, the reader.

You are presently the reader, but also the screenwriter. With every stroke of inhalation, you compose a sequel to *Life*. Will it be categorized as a hilarious sitcom, a suspense thriller, or a dramatic letdown?

My prayer is that your motion picture will characterize the temperament of God's only son, Jesus Christ, the one who died on Calvary for your sins that you might be saved. With Him on stage of *Life*, your story will merit a four star, award winning best picture.

Sincerely,

Sherri D. Dyson

P.S. *And the Lord answered me, and said, Write the vision, and make it plain upon tables, that he may run that readeth it. For the vision is yet for an appointed time, but at the end it shall speak, and not lie: though it tarry, wait for it; because it will surely come, it will not tarry* (Habakkuk 2:2-3).

FOREWORD
BY DR. MIKE MURDOCK

Sherri D. Dyson will make a poem lover out of you...I promise. One of the most unforgettable women I've ever met is Sherri D. Dyson.

Vibrant.

Compassionate.

Focused.

Sensitive.

Beautiful.

Sherri is so versatile as a minister's wife...minister of music (unsurpassed)...and a godly woman who carries the presence of the Holy Spirit around her.

When I read her poems, I recognized an uncommon gift to create a river of love, memories, and feelings...within seconds. Every human on earth should read *Can't Stop Love*.

This is a book you'll want to give to those who are the special ones of your life. It is a privilege to recommend the writings of Sherri D. Dyson.

INTRODUCTION
BY PASTOR TIMOTHY J. DYSON

When my wife asked me to introduce her in this book, I thought, Sure, that will be easy. However, the problem came when I was told I had just one page. You see, it's impossible to tell you about Sherri on one page...because she is volumes.

You will feel you know her after you share in reading her thoughts. If you want to know her a little better, order her music and feel the rhythm of her spirit. Dance to the heartbeat of her creativity. The multi-faceted Sherri just keeps going and going and going. But unlike the Eveready battery-powered toys, which are merely echoes, Sherri is a voice empowered by the Holy Spirit.

The poems and inspirations in this book are all experiences Sherri has had with me or her family, friends, and oh, don't forget the cats! Above all, her words reflect her relationship with the precious Holy Spirit.

The name of this book is *Can't Stop Love*. If you have experienced it, you know that is true. If you haven't, you will feel love as you read from the pages of Sherri's heart. And when you turn the last page and close this book, keep it near so you can allow a certain poem to speak to you again or get that inspiration for the season you are in. You will know that not only can you not stop Sherri, but you can't stop love.

PART 1

Together In The Heart

Love

- Lifetime Commitment
- Can't Stop Love
- Language Of Love
- Love Of My Life
- Perfect Fit
- Make Believe World
- One Of A Kind
- Discovering You, Discovering Me
- Together In The Heart

Love. What is love? For millenniums, this question has interrogated man's sense of reason. No doubt, at some point in your daily diary you have journalized the wonder of love.

Love is commonly confused with physical attraction toward one of the opposite sex, or love at first sight when experiencing the sting of electrifying chemistry from face to face introductions. Sexual intimacy repeatedly falls under the name of love, based on hands of clam and wham, bam, thank you ma'am.

Nevertheless, physical attraction, electrifying chemistry, and sexual intimacy are simply expressions of love. **True love is far more than impassioned conceptions, but rather a lifetime commitment to another person or being.**

My belief system describes three stages of love; puppy love, new love, and mature love.

STAGE ONE
PUPPY LOVE

Take a moment to mosey down memory lane with your childhood crush. Any second now you may resemble shades of red, as I did...

"Pucker up," I heard him say, "Your kiss is on the way." In the twinkling of an eye, we smooched and said "Good-bye." Needless to say, I haven't seen him since that day. And so the story of my eighth year, when I fell head over heels in love. I call this stage puppy love. Puppy love is merely a passing fancy of gushy fondness toward another gender. However, school-girl besottedness may stairstep onto the second stage of love if properly nourished.

STAGE TWO
NEW LOVE

New love is caught between two extremes: puppy love and mature love. A roller coaster ride typifies rocky mountains and plunging valleys strategically positioned within the heart of this vicinity. While numerous amusement parks roundabout town offset love's ups and downs, rest areas encourage R&R before traveling too far.

On the road again, shortcuts are obstructed in lieu of couples under construction. Even so, tenacious travelers of two continue in hot pursuit of mature love.

STAGE THREE
MATURE LOVE

Mature lovers invoke qualities within their partner, and seek clues to discover attributes underlying shortcomings of their better half. They follow the trail of love while climbing highlands of relationship bliss, and decidedly love when gullies become deep and wide. Awhile back, I became nostalgic with my husband, Timothy J. Dyson (Tim), about our adventurous tour from new love to mature love. We agreed that during the embryonic steps of our journey, we were very impressionable and eager to please. At times we were thrown for a loop by actions of the other, but believed ingredients of time and charm would sculpt one another into a made-to-order mate.

I recall when Tim paid attention to lack of organization within my daily routine. He tactfully approached the subject, saying, "Sherri, one of us will have to change and become more orderly." I cut to the chase with a surprise reply, "Baby, you better start changing!"

We've shared lots of laughs over dialogue the duo exchanged that day, and admit to a fault of mutual consent. Ordering our private world, we've endeavored to rearrange our to do list since tying the knot, but still stand in need of prayer, and admonish all to pray without ceasing!

All jest aside, consider the naked truth. As partners in crime, Tim and I pled guilty of attempting to change one another, and did our time as new love offenders. Freedom from guilt allows us to turn around and face the mirror, exercising mature love by sifting through our own imperfections with a fine-toothed comb.

The Apostle Paul deciphers love in a nutshell: *Love is patient, love is kind. It does not envy, it does not boast, it is not proud. It is not rude, it is not self-seeking, it is not easily angered, it keeps no record of wrongs. Love does not delight in evil, but rejoices with the truth. It always protects, always trusts, always hopes, always perseveres. Love never fails* (I Corinthians 13:4-8 NIV).

It is my persuasion that Paul labeled love as *Lifetime Commitment.*

CAN'T STOP LOVE

Stop the visits face to face
But you can't stop our love
It won't erase

Stop the glance that brings romance
But you can't stop our love
It shall enhance

Stop the kiss of lovers' lips
But you can't stop our love
Our kiss is sealed

Stop the touch of lovers' hands
But you can't stop our love
Upon command

Stop the words from being said
But you can't stop our love
It grows instead

Stop the song from being sung
But you can't stop our love
The song's begun

Our hearts are survivors of pain
Though we walk through the fire
Our love now proclaims

You can't stop our love from bringing smiles
You can't stop our love from traveling miles

Securing what we are
Embracing from afar
Keeping us together while apart

You can't stop the love within our hearts

LANGUAGE OF LOVE

We speak a different language
Interpreted by love
We fit so well together
A hand in a glove
We know each other's thoughts
Without saying a word
The language that we speak
Only true lovers have heard

We learned to speak this language
By giving of ourselves
Preferring one another
A true lover's test
Daily sacrificing
For flesh of my flesh
Heavenly expression
Of our love at its best

The language that we speak was once broken
Unclear to ears and hard to understand
But now we stand with confident assurance
We're understood within this lovers' land

It's the language of love
Sent from above
Spoken with a tender touch
Expressed in a hug
It's the language of love
Written in our eyes
Fluently pronouncing love
That can't be denied

The language of love

LOVE OF MY LIFE

You are the love of my life
You are the song of my soul
You are the light in the darkest night
You are the colorful rainbow

Sweeping across the sky of my life
Promising joy through cloudy skies
You are the laughter in my eyes
You are the love of my life

PERFECT FIT

A picture perfect puzzle
Is missing a part
The missing piece was crafted
To mend my broken heart

I lost it when you left me
You left me standing there
Please come home to me
My heart needs repair

Though you are still found missing
You're wanted in my heart
Remembering us kissing
Is tearing me apart

I long to see your smiling face
Your smiling face appear
Complete this lovers' puzzle
And make the picture clear

You're the perfect fit
For a heart like this
You fit into place
Complete the smiling face

You were special made
For my heart's design
Come and take your rightful place
In this heart of mine

You're the perfect fit

MAKE BELIEVE WORLD

In the heart of a girl
Was a make believe world

In the mind of a child
Was a fairy tale

Though I'm growing older
I still believe it's true

In the heart of me
It was you

ONE OF A KIND

Your magical smile
Stands out in a crowd
Beaming at me
For all eyes to see

When I'm feeling down
You pose as my clown
To bring out my best
Ignoring the rest

You're one of a kind
Uniquely designed with me in mind
You're one of a kind
Perfected by hands of love divine

To fit in my heart
And never depart from my life
You're one of a kind
Completely defined in my eyes

DISCOVERING YOU DISCOVERING ME

You took me by complete surprise
When you came into my life

My fantasies and wildest dreams
Have finally come to light

Mysterious discovery
Unfolds before my eyes

We'll go down in history
The case of you and I

I've searched the whole world over
To find the missing clue

Proof of love that never ends
The evidence is you

Discovering a lover
I've found a hand to hold

Discovering a friendship
Where all my dreams are told

Discovering a love
More precious than gold

That can't be bought or sold
It never grows old

Discovering you discovering me

TOGETHER IN THE HEART

I sit here silently
Wondering where you are

I love you endlessly
You are my shining star

Vividly my dreams take me to your arms
Silently assuring we will never part

Though we're apart
We're together in the heart

Your smile says to me
I love you more than words can say

You touch me tenderly
Taking me far away

From a distance I can hear you whispering my name
Giving me the strength to face another day

Knowing that we
Are together in the heart

Together in the heart
Holding hands from afar

Together in the heart
Your lips meet mine and never part

Though we are physically apart
We are forever together in the heart

PART 2

Triking By Trees

Children

- Heirloom Memories
- Innocence

HEIRLOOM MEMORIES

Cruising home after a hectic day at the office, I generally scan AM/FM radio stations in search of uplifting music or clean-cut talk shows underscoring current events. At close of this particular day I skipped past the legendary voice of the late Nat King Cole, when my sense of hearing detected a sweet-sounding female voice accompanying him on the classic song, *Unforgettable*. Immediately tuning back the dial, I became spellbound by symphonious sounds making melody over the airwaves. Clear as a bell, the radio personality announced the release of the single, *Unforgettable*. Dubbing feminine tones with the previously recorded voice of her father, Natalie Cole made her heirloom memory simply...unforgettable.

Years later, while shuffling through time-worn paraphernalia, I stumbled across an age-old piece of paper bearing original poetry in the hand of my grandfather, the late Rev. T. P. Johnson. Thumbing through his self-reliant versification, I took into account how time and again he transcribed affectionate thoughts about his wife, Ila Mae, and the adventures of their three musketeers, Barbara Jean, Elizabeth S., and Tommy Dewayne.

Meditations Of A Loving Father, the hand-inscribed poem penned on the heels of the birth of his only son, brought attention to his tenderness toward children. Reproducing scribbled imagination of Grandfather, I interwove my sentiments with his to compose *Innocence*, a ballad giving prominence to clear-conscienced children.

Innocence will maintain life as an inscription to the word painter who practiced interpretive language of the inner soul. His heart-thoughts established heirloom memories that classify me as a wealthy, young heiress.

Heirloom memories. One may wonder, what does this symbolize? Allow me to elucidate Webster's definition of words *heir* (male), *heiress* (female), *heirloom*, and *memory*. An heir or heiress is described as a person who inherits, while heirloom means a family possession. Broken down, the word memory is something remembered. Put two and two together and the terms heirloom and memory represent a person who inherits a family possession as something remembered.

Until recently, I have perceived an heir or heiress as one laying claim to articles of monetary value. However, they are unmistakenly identified as persons who inherit family possessions, with no mention of pocketbook keepsakes. As a result, memories legislate a family possession, which designate future generations to glimmer from the past, assuming far more than monumental superstructures or bank accounts.

Heirloom memories may be tangible as the song *Unforgettable* and the ballad *Innocence*, or intangible as precious gems stored within the nest egg of the inner man. In any event, things remembered will continually download to a computer program in a league of its own: the mind of humanity. **Majestic buildings will deteriorate, savings accounts may deplete, but heirloom memories will preserve authenticity of the unforgotten one.**

INNOCENCE

Sherri D. Dyson
& the late Rev. T. P. Johnson

Beautiful feet that patter all about
What music so sweet
How I love to hear that sound
Of innocent legs running all the day
Carrying children outside to play
Innocent mouth, innocent hands
Miracles formed at God's command

Beautiful hair tousled all about
A picture so fair
Drawn by God there is no doubt
Of innocent smiles laughing all the day
I pray for a while He'll keep them that way
Innocent fears, innocent tears
Given a toy will disappear

Innocent children, innocent minds
With no thought of being mean
Their minds are pure and clean
Innocent children, innocent eyes
Dancing to a lullaby
There's never a disguise
Innocent lives

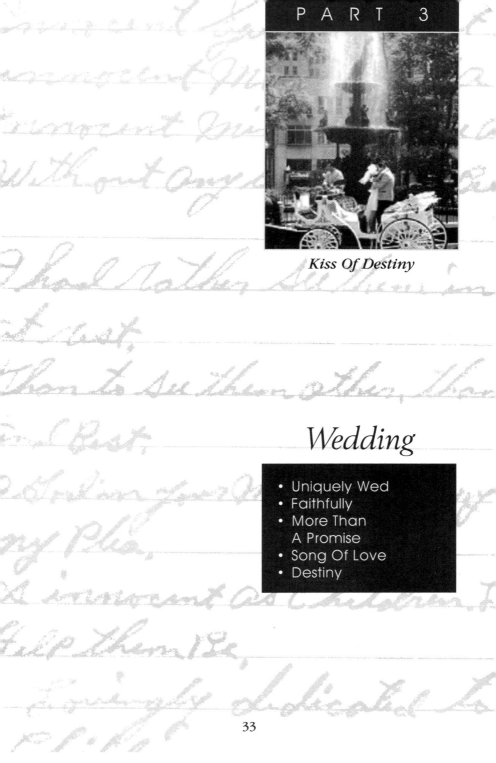

PART 3

Kiss Of Destiny

Wedding

- Uniquely Wed
- Faithfully
- More Than
  A Promise
- Song Of Love
- Destiny

July 2, 1994, opened the third chapter of my book of life entitled, *Uniquely Wed*.

Traveling from The Peabody Hotel, Memphis, Tennessee, I overheard ballads of Kenny G. drifting from Court Square, three blocks away. Set in motion by a white horse towing a chariot lined with plush blue interior, I caught wind of Mariah Carey effortlessly serenading a sea of enthusiastic cheers with the pop tune, *Vision of Love*.

As I rode toward a gazebo designed for those of noble rank, white doves fluttered above my head, while black-hooved feet deliberately galloped at breakneck speed toward my artistocratic prince. Regally escaping his chariot enroute to rescue me from mine, my knight in shining armor gazed into windows of the soul of destiny.

Standing to attention in the presence of God, family, and friends, we solemnly pledged to become an honorable extension of one another by joining forces to obey a mandate decreed by the royal line. No longer single, but partners in ministry, we dismounted our buggy fashioned for one to board a jetliner destined for the city that never sleeps.

Flight attendants welcomed us with quiet wishes for newlywed bliss, directing us to the first class section reserved for two. Safety signs exhausted, we burst forth toward our upward flight featuring a ceiling of sky blue. A few hours slipped by before we awoke to the pilot's proclamation blasting from the cockpit, *prepare for landing*.

Preparation for descent onto the runway of our future consisted of selecting an entree from the Master Chef's choice of the day earmarked revival in the land.

Quick as the wind, landing gear met the face of ground and taxied directly to the Lord's Palace. Much to our fulfillment, children of the Lord escorted us to a honeymoon ball held in the cathedral of preeminence where the King served from the Master's table seating the royal priesthood.

Accepting our appointment as the King's anointed, we sang psalms with the congregation of those in divine right, and exhorted the multitude of believers who worshipped His Royal Highness. Declaring splendor of His majesty to unbelievers of His Lordship, our assignment was in full swing.

Seven years later, we agree that stateliness within the empire has revealed our seventh heaven, while premiering our school of hard knocks. On the other hand, we've come bearing good tidings: the former outweighs the latter.

Our noble commitment is to remain true to vows of the best sort, those between man and wife, and to promote the bestseller inspired by the King of kings, for as long as we both shall live.

FAITHFULLY

I love you
With every breath I take
I hold you
With every step I make
I'm lost in your embrace
In dreams I can't escape
'Cause love has come and there is no mistake

I need you
The silent strength you bring
I want you
You're every woman's dream
So baby don't delay
Come carry me away
Confident your princess now awaits

You are the one for me
And we will always be
Together, you and I
Forever faithfully

Walking hand in hand
Fulfilling Heaven's plan
Embracing life together
Securing our forever

Faithfully

MORE THAN A PROMISE

Promises today are spoken
Wedding rings signify a token
Of love that's just begun
Two lives becoming one

There are no words to say to tell you
But these hands of clay will show you
Forever you will see
This love inside of me

More than a promise
I give to you my life
More than a promise
I vow to hold you tight

More than a promise
I'll follow you into the darkest night
More than a promise
I'll love you till I die

SONG OF LOVE

I memorize the lyrics
Written in your eyes
And recognize the music
As endless love unites
Drifting from your heart to mine

I hear the sound of laughter
Within the tune that's played
Happy everafter
Beginning here today
As we harmonize as one

With the lyrics in your eyes
The rhythm in your heartbeat
The song comes alive

With the tune in your voice
The music in your laughter
The song never dies

The song of love

DESTINY

I see you standing there
Time stands still
Reflecting love
Our hearts once concealed

We walk hand in hand
Through the opened door
Cherishing the love
Destiny has bore

I've found my destiny
This moment in time
Forever *my love*
You will define

Destiny

I stand in awe
At my discovery
Our lives are joined
In perfect harmony

Composed in a song
Written by God above
The music is coming together
This song will last forever

We've found our destiny
This moment in time
Together *my love*
We will define

Destiny

PART 4

Faraway Look
By The Brook

Last Goodbye

- Hand Crocheted Booties
- Love Stories
- Love's Legacy

HAND CROCHETED BOOTIES
In remembrance of the late Irene G. Motes.

As a young woman of 19, I received sobering news that my grandmother had drawn her last breath. Moved to tears, my thoughts sprinted cross-country to numerous lives affected by her 76-year voyage on God's green earth.

As mother of ten boys and two girls, grandmother of 37 grandchildren, and great grandmother of 36 great grandchildren, her far-reaching influence penetrated the roots of her lineage. **Her light-heartedness whispered merriment to individuals given the opportunity to tread upon her pathway of life**. She expected to be cheerful, and transferred happiness to others in the process of her joy.

All through childhood, I would count down days before traveling to Grandma's house for Christmas each year. Although she resided in a humble abode, and survived on a minimal amount of income, I could rely on Grandma to present me with a singular box bearing the name, Sherri. The most cherished presents were hand crocheted booties that took form by signature design of her aging hands.

When fully acquainted with a day in the life of an adult, I faced the question, how did Grandma managed to purchase individual Christmas gifts for 85 immediate family members year after year? Voicing the subject of investigation, I discovered the inside story of how she budgeted a small amount to apply toward the holiday kitty monthly, faithfully ensuring her offspring a personalized token of love from the lady of many titles.

Insight into the story assured me, it's not the quality of Grandma's gifts that survive her, but rather the quantity of undying hugs that live in her love.

LOVE STORIES

Through the years we've left a legacy
Entitled *How to Love*
It was written from experience
By hands that wrote as one

Though mistakes were made
With just one glance the editor revised
The final draft that ends today
But keeps our love alive

We've established the ingredients
For making love that lasts
An ounce of smiles will travel miles
If sprinkled with a dash

Of respect for one another
And a pinch of honesty
Prepared within a lifetime
For all to taste and see

Keep telling stories about our love
Don't let it end
Let it go down in history
Our legacy

Keep telling stories about our love
Let it descend
Down to the children beneath your knee
Our legacy

LOVE'S LEGACY

With each individual life
There's a legacy to find

It may not be for eyes to see
But in the hearts of girls like me

It doesn't live inside a home
But only in the heart alone

So when *my love* is dead and gone
I'll stand alone with love that's grown

From all the joy that we have shared
Day by day and through the years

PART 5

Baptized At Four

Spiritual

- S.T.O.P. See The Overall Picture
- His Purpose In Me
- The Battlefield Of My Mind
- Questions And Answers
- Stop The Insanity
- Face In A Crowd
- Eyes Unseen
- My Favorite Place
- Praise Anyway
- Please Understand
- From Emptiness To Fullness
- The One My Heart Loves
- By My Side
- Images
- Giving Away My Pain
- Godly Thoughts

S.T.O.P. - SEE THE OVERALL PICTURE

STOP: See the overall picture flashed into my sleeping brain like a marquee advertising stop signs. Awakened from a deep slumber, I stumbled into our home office where Tim was downloading *you've got mail.* I groggily derailed his e-mail train of thought to introduce my stop sign revelation. His response boosted my ego to keep me elevated for hours to come.

Light of day brought me to a screeching halt to view the bright red octagon strategically posted on every corner of my heart, directing me to stop. Immediately blocking all two-legged traffic from the white linen-draped French door leading into my orange office, I sank into my high-back royal blue suede chair. Positioned behind a brushed gold glass-topped desk, I was humorously reminded of Tim's initial reaction to my nonconforming office decor.

Embryo stages of my tangerine office invention depicted a Halloween party in the middle of summer, according to his mind's eye. Combining vibrant shades of yellow, orange, red, purple and blue spelled mismatch in the spelling bee of TJD (Timothy J. Dyson). Nevertheless, his perception lacked the overall picture of the product of my imagination...

Florida banana trees housing squealing monkeys swinging from limb to limb, talking parrots that mimic inspired words, ribbiting frogs to welcome guests while startling intruders, apes decked out in kelly green Hawaiian Tee-shirts singing *Great Balls of Fire*, and potted sunflowers blurting out *You Are My Sunshine* boldly fade into the backdrop of the final concoction called *Sherri's Office*.

Much to my surprise, my descriptive design now exists as Tim's most popular showpiece. His mannerisms remind me of Tom Hanks' character in the movie *Big*, when he entertains our guests by hunting the orange jungle for clever trinkets that deliver a few laughs.

The slip and fall of topsy turvy days periodically suggest I shut up shop to take stock of God's unique idea: me. When I pause to stare back at the reflected image of me, myself, and I, I occasionally bear semblance to a bare, orange room lacking innovation. My initial reaction often resembles Tim's first response to my office. In any case, as the Artist of all artists takes the first step to examine possibilities of my existence, the sketch of my being slowly begins to set the tone for the overall picture of His purpose in me.

Take a moment to unhurriedly canvass the richness of your life's portrait painted by the Master's hand. Once perfected, He guarantees a one of a kind masterpiece in a class of its own. His priceless piece of artistry will exhibit unparalleled colors of the overall picture viewed as *you*.

HIS PURPOSE IN ME

The Father's plan
Unknown to man
Revealed in ways I sometimes
Don't understand

Refining me
So I can be
A picture of His purpose
And plan for me

A masterpiece created
By the Father's hands
A drawing of my life
The finished product stands

To be seen through the eyes of the Father
Who sees in me what I could be
Revealing His purpose in me

This work of art
Drawn on my heart
Shows me which direction
I need to start

To do the things
That seem to be
Impossible to me
But then I see

The colors of my life
Stand before me now
A picture perfect rainbow
Promising this vow

That someday I'll understand each mile
Is finishing this masterpiece
Revealing His purpose in me

THE BATTLEFIELD OF MY MIND
Elizabeth Motes & Sherri D. Dyson

There's a battle that is raging
No peace within to find
Forming an army within me
Battling in my mind

Each day begins new battles
Of conflict and despair
Creating new dimensions
Of war that seems unfair

As morning sun arises
I grope to find a way
To gather ammunition
To battle through this day

By kneeling down before Him
I stand with strength to fight
Prepared with holy armor
Erect as Heaven's knight

Prayer becomes my weapon
The Word, a two edged sword
I charge into the battle
To reap a great reward

As enemies slain before me
Are trampled beneath my feet
I raise the victory banner
To never sound retreat

As sunset falls behind me
With satan's army bound
Confidence consumes me
Through His spirit found

As Heaven's host rejoices
Encamped around my soul
I have no fear within me
'Cause God is in control

QUESTIONS AND ANSWERS

Life is a question
Where is the answer?
Life is a puzzle
Where are the pieces?

Life is a song
What is the melody?
Life is a story
What is the ending?

Some questions will never be answered
Some pieces will never be found
Some songs will never have music
But life will end to all those around

Look to your Maker
For answers today
He'll pick up the pieces
Write lyrics that say

I am your beginning
And ending too
The thunder of music
And Heaven's the tune

STOP THE INSANITY
Sherri D. Dyson & Timothy J. Dyson

People running everywhere
No one takes the time to care
Living separate hectic lives
Socializing through the night

Keeping up with Misses Jones
Flaunting what we call our own
No time to make our house a home
Living for ourselves alone

People hurting everywhere
Begging us to stop and care
Living separate lonely lives
Sadly crying through the night

Setting our priorities straight
We need to recognize their state
Stop and take a look around
Let the grace of God abound

Abortion clinics everywhere
Killing babies, they don't care
Aborting infants everyday
Unborn to man and thrown away

Stop and listen for the cry
Of unborn babies made to die
We must take the time to pray
Allow the child a chance to play

Rape and killing everywhere
Alcohol and drugs to spare
Increasing violence every day
Riots breaking in L.A.

Missing children gone from home
Parents wonder if they're grown
Divorce is on an uphill climb
Statistics say that love's a lie

A rising rate of suicide
They don't care if they live or die
They leave the family wondering why
All that they can do is cry

Leaving children home alone
Free to roam the streets unknown
Investing time within their lives
Pays interest till the day they die

Stop the insanity
Focus in on what is right
Stop the insanity
See the teardrops in their eyes
Wiped away there's no disguise
When looking through the Father's eyes
Insanity must take a bow

FACE IN A CROWD

Watching people in this place
They've come here from every race
Some are blonde
Some are red
Some are brunette
Some are even turning gray

I begin to wonder out loud
Am I just another face in a crowd?
When they look at me
Do they really see
God's love or do they see a frown?

A teen-age couple holding hands
They're already making plans
A baby cries
A mother sighs
And throws up her hands
A father's chest begins to expand

I wonder if the smile on my face
Spreads the love of Jesus in this place
When they look at me
Do they really see
More than just another face?

EYES UNSEEN

Eyes unseen
Are all around
Discovering faults
I've not yet found

Exposed by those
Who often conclude
I am a lie
Masked with truth

I'm rarely amazed
By what they observe
They're just an opinion
Of many on earth

Talking aloud
They frequently speak
Tearing down others
So they'll look complete

Leave it to God
Alone to judge
With unseen eyes
Of sovereign love

He will reveal
What ought to be seen
And grace will conceal
The rest of me

MY FAVORITE PLACE

I love to go walking in the rain
To feel raindrops falling on my face

I love to build a snowman
After blizzards come

But I've yet to find my favorite place
Except in God alone

I found my favorite place
In His arms of love

I found a happy face
Wrapped up in His grace

The favorite place
That I am speaking of

Is a place where all are welcome
Won't you come and join me in my favorite place?

PRAISE ANYWAY

In the heart of my soul
In the depth of my life
In the breath of my days
I'm gonna praise

In the laughter that's lost
In the teardrops that fall
In the sorrow I know
I'm gonna praise

I'm gonna praise God anyway
No matter what I face today
I'm gonna praise God anyway
No matter what may come my way

I'm gonna praise

PLEASE UNDERSTAND

He was left with just one dollar
Yet the circumstances lingered
His children left with little to survive

With no promise for tomorrow
And a pocket full of pennies
He bowed his head and breathed a humble sigh

He said...

Please understand my need
Please sow compassion's seed
Please show His love to me
Unconditionally
Understand my need

She was left without a partner
When he chose a different pathway
To leave a trail of memories in her mind

Discarded and rejected
By the one who pledged forever
Reality was left with no disguise

She said...

Please understand my need
Please sow compassion's seed
Please show His love to me
Unconditionally
Understand my need

FROM EMPTINESS TO FULLNESS

Entangled in a battle
Confined within a heartache

Looking for a shadow
Of hope in sight

Emptiness engulfs me
Sadness won't subside

Embarking on a journey
From emptiness to fullness

With tiny steps I'm learning
To lean on Him

For daily confirmation
Of perfect love in action

I find fulfillment
In the eyes of the one called *Love*

I find fulfillment
In the arms of the Lamb of God

THE ONE MY HEART LOVES

Just like a falling star
He fell into my heart
Shooting down from the sky
He brightened up my nights

The one my heart loves
Fulfills my desire
He compliments my style

He perfectly synchronized
The dream I visualized
Picturesque as a rose
Blooming dreams unfold

The one my heart loves
With passionate fire
Consumes me with delight

The one my heart loves
Sees the best in me
The one my heart loves
Is my living dream

Awaking my soul
Brave and bold
Charging into my life

The one my heart loves
Jesus Christ

BY MY SIDE

Some will walk away
Others disappear
Leave without a trace
In the night

But I can count on you
When my friends are gone
You will always be
By my side

Some will tear me down
Others whisper lies
Slaughtering my heart
Like a knife

But I can count on you
When my friends are gone
You will always be
By my side

You are my friend
Even when I fail
You will always be
By my side

IMAGES

Images reflected
In mirrors all around
Easily rejected
She must fit in the crowd
The trends are set
They've all been met
Will happiness be found?

Anorexic illness
Kills without a sound
Weight awareness haunts her
Daily losing pounds
She wants to sleep
And never eats
Don't ignore the signs

She must obtain the image
Projected in her mind
She thinks she looks distorted
Disease has made her blind
Can't you hear the silent cry
Spoken from her eyes?

Won't somebody help me?
I'm dying from inside
Say you won't reject me
Because I'm oversized
I need someone to understand
The thoughts within my mind

We've got to save her from herself
Reflect the love of God above
Save her from herself
Project the image of His love
Give her food for thought so she can eat

We've got to save her from herself
Feed her manna from the Word
Save her from herself
Tell her that her voice is heard
Desperation speaks distinctively

Save her from herself

GIVING AWAY MY PAIN

I'm giving away
All of my pain
I'm bringing to you
All of my shame

'Cause you bore the cross
To bury my fear
I'm giving away my pain

GODLY THOUGHTS

Have you given God a thought lately?

Have you worshipped His Majesty,
or do rocks cry beneath your feet?

When the Pharisees asked Jesus
to silence His disciples from lifting
their voices in a loud praise,
He replied, *"I tell you, If they keep quiet,
the stones will cry out."* (Luke 19:40 NIV).

Has a round stone replaced your song?

Skyscraper trees, sway with the breeze,
worshipping the King,
won't you join in and sing?

PART 6

Pregnant With Preston

Seasonal

- Springtime Flower Frostbitten By Winter Chill
- Special Delivery
- Seasons Of Life
- Creating World
- Moon's Eye

69

SPRINGTIME FLOWER FROSTBITTEN
BY WINTER CHILL

Darkness engulfed me as I shivered from the winter chill that frostbit the lifeblood of expectancy that occupied my being. Symbolically speaking, I needed immediate attention from Doctor Jesus, but I was listening intently to my OB/GYN who offered little or no comfort with his words, "I don't see a baby."

Only three months earlier while visiting my parents for a few days had I noticed a significant change in the way I physically felt. I was extremely fatigued and experiencing dizziness periodically. Food cravings forbidden for low-fat queens, such as cheeseburgers, french fries, and chocolate milk, were unquenchable. My Mother's woman's intuition prompted me to visit a local doctor to determine the answer to the million dollar question, "Could I be pregnant?"

With a prior medical diagnosis of a female condition referred to as Endometriosis, and several years of keeping E.P.T. Home Pregnancy Tests in business only to receive a negative response, my expectancy level was at an all time low when the nurse announced with gusto, "You're pregnant!"

About that time my ever busy cellular rang apprising me of Tim's addiction to the telephone. From the stirrups of the examining room I enthusiastically exclaimed, "Our dream's alive!" I remember his response like yesterday, "Can you find out what it is today?" I gently reminded him of the four month waiting period for determining the gender of our baby, but quickly assured him that we would share in the excitement of this experience as soon as the occasion presented itself.

AT&T joined us in the early stages of celebrating our baby's conception by presenting us with a long distance bill exclusive enough to be sent as pregnancy announcements. Everybody from Uncle Ben to Aunt Earnistine was notified of the springtime flower taking sprout in my womb.

The fragrance of our tiny rose led me to the mall where a forty dollar shopping spree bought several *How To Be A Great Mom* books, and stocked our shelves with unique names for our one of a kind child-to-be. We desperately wished for a girl and carefully scanned each page to determine her initials, C.N.D., representing Courtney Nicole Dyson. During this dramatic scene of parental preparation, a boy was nameless.

For ninety days I impatiently examined the reflection of our little one's abode, and was elated to recognize that expansions were finally under construction and were built large enough to fill maternity clothes bought for the debut of my Mother-to-be news flash. The black and white jacket with the matching black expandable skirt fit snugly over our pea in a pod.

I rose to meet the challenge of an expectant Mother by familiarizing myself with the different stages my body would undergo while in waiting. Tim and I watched together as our unborn offspring grew from conception to eleven weeks, and read of how developing eyes, arms, legs, and one tiny heart tightly knit with ours, were in the making.

At twelve weeks we were escorted from the waiting room into the examining room to anticipate the thump, thump of a palpitating drum called the heartbeat of baby Dyson. With sweating palms clenched together, and eyes anxiously glued to one another, we listened, and listened, and listened, and...

"I want an ultrasound immediately!" the Doctor ordered. In an attempt to diffuse the explosive situation at hand he quickly explained the remote possibility that the inception of pregnancy could have been sooner or later than originally determined, but to no avail.

Without delay the ultrasound was performed, displaying an image of emptiness undefined in our unrehearsed stage show. Tim quietly observed as I choked out words not written in my script, "Where's the baby?" It seemed as if an unnamed villain was sabotaging the screenplay of our dream.

What seemed to be days, passed in twenty-four hours. Numerous diagnostic test and observatory x-rays revealed a definite answer to medical technicians, but posed an indefinite question to us, "Was our dream still alive?"

The doctor's report transferred us from the freshness of a springtime shower into the smothering horror of a winter avalanche within seconds. "How?" "How could it be that the form of our love never matured past six weeks?" "Why wouldn't God choose to bless us with the perfect little girl, named Courtney, that babbles in our carefully written drama?"

Our springtime flower wilted in death before reaching full bloom. With a wind-chill factor of twenty-nine below, winter stripped our drama of a happy ending, but reminded us that scripts aren't always written with explanations. Although postscripts sometimes follow...

P.S. Tim and Sherri Dyson announce the arrival of Preston Kendall on October 18, 2000, at 5:48 PM, weighing 7 pounds, 4 ounces and measuring 20 inches long. Preston (Old English) "From the Preacher's Estate," Kendall (Old English) "From the Bright Valley," initials P.K., "Preacher's Kid."

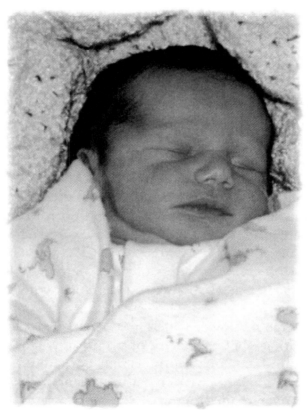

Bundle of Blue
Preston Kendall (P.K.)

The real life drama was far greater than the imaginary ending, because when God writes the post script He dots all I's and crosses all T's!

SPECIAL DELIVERY

The man child
Delivered from my womb
Holds my heart in his hands
With every childish tune

He captures the kid in me
With every game we play
And leaves me longing for his smile
Whenever I'm away

I thought I wanted a little girl
Who looked a lot like me
Until the day I met my son
By special delivery

I look into his eyes
And see his daddy living there
And recognize the nose as mine
Upon his face so fair

I often wonder if he's an angel
Dressed up in disguise
For me to snuggle every day
Nurture and to guide

I hear him cry and cradle him close
To my milky motherhood
To nestle with my tiny gift
As only Mother should

I watch him sleeping through the night
So peaceful and serene
And pray that God will keep him safe
Until the daylight beams

I know that God will hear my prayer
Whispered through the night
Because He listens close to moms
Who hold His babies tight

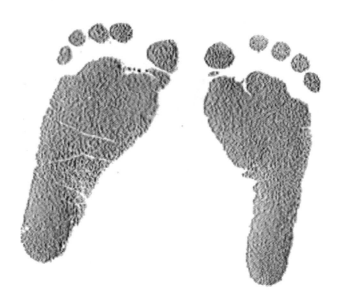

SEASONS OF LIFE

Seasons of life
Laughter and sorrow
They're all entwined in the same

Springtime and summer
Autumn and winter
Bringing forth seasons of change

Seasons of life
Born to creation
They're all confined by the days

Autumn leaves falling
Strip me of beauty
But there's a reason for the change

Change me
Beautiful spring
Water the flowers from the rain

Change me
Rearrange me
So the season's not in vain

CREATING WORLD

A brush of green
Falling on the leaves
Creating world

As gentle breezes blow
The flowers start to grow
Creating world

A shade of blue
Sweeping 'cross the sky
Creating world

The ocean meets the sand
Then rushes back again
Creating world

Master creator
Artist at work
Poetry in motion
Rhythmic words
Creating world

MOON'S EYE

The moon overlooks the floor of humanity
Spotlighting filthiness of the unkept
Zooming in on the elite of the immaculate

Is my inner being
viewed as a dirty kitchen parlor gone unswept...
Or a freshly polished coffee table
spotlessly reflecting the light?

Ask yourself this question...
Which one am I in the moon's eye?

PART 7

Black Tail Affair

Animal Lovers

- Nine Lives Times Three
- Curious Creatures

Growing from kittens to cats, Tiger, Dominoe, and Boots are a trio of distinct personalities and fluffy coats. With the decorative theme of my home portraying an African Safari, their coats of many colors blend exotically with the leopard, zebra, and cow rugs that furbish floors throughout their territory, my house.

The extrovert of the bunch would be Tiger, the guard cat. Bearing stripes for his namesake, Tiger is a spitting image of his descent. The firstborn of three, he guards his turf with the eye of a tiger. Whenever another four-legged creature ventures to tread upon his domain, he violently lunges toward his prey, often to receive a great awakening when he comes face to face with his match.

Tiger has assembled a collection of lizards, captured from what he considers his outside kingdom, that he secretly stores beneath the sofa with sinful pride, like the cat that swallowed a canary. Much to my horror, he frequently shows off his prized possessions, then struts his stuff with tail held high.

Tiger demands attention 24/7, and pouts whenever he suspects he's shy of his share. Posing as the door greeter, he often reciprocates idle chitchat with a hospitable meow. In human vernacular, Tiger is the speaker of the house.

Dominoe, the second addition to the Dyson family, resembles a snow white polar bear, flaunting a tail of black. The exact opposite of Tiger, he is a cat of few meows and timid mannerisms. His unnameable words are uttered as squeaks, while his vibrating purrs imitate the sound of a moving freight train. With an easygoing temperament, it requires little effort to quiet his demands. However, shedding his backward demeanor and standing his ground is not out of character.

No scaredy cat by any means. He has sauntered away from a cat fight as champion on more than one occasion, covering his tracks with the aire of the cock of the walk.

The omega of the pack is the people cat. Sporting a tailor-made black and white fur jacket, and assuming the disposition of a lamb, he took a pussyfoot trot down the alley leading to my change of heart the instant he traipsed onto our church property, disdaining my written permission.

With two animals pumping a bloodline originating from the African dominion presently populating my comfy-cozy habitat, I adamantly asserted I would not adopt another twin species. However, caught off guard, I soon became a victim of a sneak attack when the unexpected church cat pounced on the grounds of my sensibility, digging up a buried soft spot carefully blocked off from his kind.

I submitted to the catcall once and for all the moment Tim, who was previously of the opinion to eliminate all cats from our hearth and home, tiptoed into my office carrying, guess who! He said, "Sherri, this the most beautiful kitten I've ever laid eyes on. What do you think about giving him a warm bed?"

My resistance broken down, I suffered a heart attack by a kitten turned cat named Boots. Snug as a bug in a rug, he redefines the term lap-cat at any given opportunity.

The Tiger and Dominoe duo grew into a trio soon after I selected the accompaniment of Boots the caboose. **Voicing their individual differences, they blend in trained unison ninety percent of the time**. Although, every now and then one will change their tune, defending his jurisdiction to the beat of a different drum.

To copycat a band of pots and pans, Tiger, Dominoe, and Boots whoop and holler lyrics expressing playful curiosity, purring contentment, and meowing misbehavior, to name a few. Take your pick; it's listed in the repertoire of nine lives times three.

CURIOUS CREATURES

At work or at play
My life is amazed
Laughing at cats
And how they behave

I am their master
By day and by night
Often patrolling
And breaking up fights

They live in my home
But often will roam
To unforeseen places
Where they don't belong

When bathing themselves
They'll sit in my chair
Licking their fur
And missing no hair

Whenever they're finished
They'll usually sleep
On top of each other
Piled in a heap

Curious creatures
Creeping at night
Pouncing on lizards
With gleeful delight

Marking their turf
They'll look for a mouse
When none can be found
They often will pout

They seem to be happy
Whenever they purr
And when they are needy
A meow will be heard

Waking me up
From sleep that is sound
Nudging my hand
With heads that are round

Rubbing against me
They speak of a love
That daily explains
What cats are made of

PART 8

Say Cheese

Mother's Day

- In The Form Of A Woman
- Woman To Woman
- My Mother, My Friend
- The One Who Dreamed Of Me
- Silent Applaud
- A Lady

IN THE FORM OF A WOMAN

The second I laid eyes on her, I recognized the flesh and blood of familiarity. Her naturalness carried the persona of a lady at ease, as she gracefully wore a sentimental grin from ear to ear, and whispered sweet nothings with the accent of a guardian angel.

For the first couple years after we met under water, my inseparable comrade filled the shoes of my favorite playmate. Whenever she tiptoed into my nursery of gibber-jabber and snooze, I would kick and giggle, sometimes even shed newborn crocodile tears, until she skillfully caught the hint and nestled with it. Affectionately picking me up, she would cradle her bundle of joy against her milky-way bosom, humming ballads that rocked as lullabies. Our unbreakable bond was so durable that even the law of gravity, embodied by heavy eyelids, could not impair her innate ability to nurture the center of attention who remained bright eyed and bushy tailed when all else slept.

As my virgin wings took flight to climb stair steps of childhood, she would intermittently recite a series of incidents that brought gaiety to my unfettered spirit. Her true to life overview, recapturing the moment she caught wind of the doctor's statement, "It's a girl," prompted me to notice the vivacious manner she described spellbinding tales of a tenderfoot named Sherri Denise in the long run of every line.

The introduction to her verbal autobiography pronounced herself tickled pink when mathematical calculations determined my ten tiny fingers, plus eight toes, seated adjacent to two little piggy's squealing wee-wee all the way home, to equal a definite twenty. Positive all principle parts were numerically computed, she took steps to get my feet wet on the playing field of fashion.

Inspecting my potential of becoming a clotheshorse, she directed a closed-club pageant by sprucing up my seven pound, four ounce physique in an array of ruffled frills that sashayed down the runway of her lap. After extensive deliberation, she ruled on the side of the Sunday go to meeting red dress, daintily accessorized with black patent leather shoes, still preserved for feminine wear within her treasure chest of memoirs.

The storybook continued the day she overheard me precisely assemble my first sentence, "My baby's so sweet," parroting the words of my mentor. That momentous event marked my toddler advance into singing lessons taught by my lifetime instructor, who adamantly recapped for emphasis, "Sherri, you've got to sing with a lot of enthusiasm!"

Borrowing from the storehouse of her mind, she recounted the day I precociously arrived on the training ground of elementary education, to bump into the woman with eyes in the back of her head. A golden opportunity had preapproved her as qualified to assume the position as my homeroom teacher, who jumped at the chance to gird my intellect with essential data on how to read, write, and behave like a lady.

When adolescents came knocking on my door, she would persistently sneak a peek through the window curtain of perception, keeping tabs on her babe in the woods, who was bursting forth into the innocent young woman she had only imagined would ultimately come to fruition.

Coming to grips with the teen-age tussle proved to be a challenge rather than threat to the resilience of her apron strings. Her opinions were readily-available instead of ready-made. Her expertise remained on-call around the clock to take part in hand-picking a well-suited outfit that would enhance the evening of my first date. At the same time, her spontaneous empathizer stayed permanently stocked with Kleenex boxes of baby-soft tissue for blotting out photographic memories developed by heartthrob suitors who had discreetly slipped through my fingers.

Pride mixed with prejudice sizzled on her homemade plate of motherhood when she endorsed the bottom line of my primary college application for enrollment into the school of music. With rapid response from the office of administration dispensing a letter of acceptance to her youngling, she donated her support by physically escorting my feet of seventeen years to the division of harmonics that majored in the sound of music.

When halls of ivy turned to aisles of wedlock, she unmasked secret droplets of water that forecast a flash-flood warning to foreshadow my open-air wedding as a national disaster area. Nevertheless, flabbergasted meteorologists were unable to save face when tears freely rushed down the drain to a heart brimming over with elation. Mother hen cracked the egg protected under her wing to catch sight of her full-grown baby chick flap wings, fly high, and come into her own, in the form of a woman.

Her present-day tale of suspense, spotlighting her thirty-two year old daughter of today, portrays her readiness to regard my indiscretions as wisdom acquired, and my fumbles as safeguard in the face of a tackle.

Her reflection in my mirror of time illuminates the image of perfection in my mind. Mother to daughter, daughter to mother, woman to woman, time will uncover the rest of the story.

To be continued...

WOMAN TO WOMAN

Woman to woman
Our worlds collide
With telephone chats
And vacation time

Befriending each other
We search for a way
To somehow rediscover
Our lives in the day

Why haven't we noticed
Today is the day
That we will conceive
New memories made

When one page is full
Another begins
Let's start a new series
That never will end

To be continued...
Leads one to mystique
Why don't we endeavor
To write as we speak

MY MOTHER, MY FRIEND

She wakes up every morning and thinks of me
Smiling at the memories of how I used to be
Kneeling in prayer
She knows the Father's there

Holding me in His arms at night
Hugging me
Holding me tight
Kissing all the hurt away
Cradling me with love

She knows that He is walking by my side
Talking with me
Smiling down so tenderly
She is now at peace
Knowing He's replacing her love

Since childhood Mother's always been a friend to me
The nurse that I would run to
Whenever I would hurt my knee
Though I'm all grown up now
Her head is humbly bowed
Thanking God for . . .

Holding me in His arms at night
Hugging me
Holding me tight
Kissing all the hurt away
Cradling me with love

She knows that He is walking by my side
Talking with me
Smiling down so tenderly
She is now at peace
Knowing He's replacing her love

A Mother's love knows no end
She's always there being a friend
Within her womb my life began
Giving birth to the love that's within
My Mother, my friend

THE ONE WHO DREAMED OF ME

She dreamed of me before I came to be
And wondered if I'd be a he or she
Would I be a baby boy with mischief in my mind
Or be a little girl with baby dolls that cry?

I looked into her eyes with wonder
And recognized her voice as Mother
Could it be she's just a dream or childhood fantasy
Or is it Mommie Dear welcoming me here?

Ever since the day she called me special
I knew that we'd become the best of friends
Her little baby girl or within her woman's world
Memories won't escape the times I've spent

With the one who dreamed of me
Before she saw my face
Visualized within her mind
A little girl with lace

The one who dreamed of me
While her womb embraced
The miracle in her eyes today

SILENT APPLAUD

As an observant child of a mother's love, I've seen with my own eyes that nothing, or no one can equal the incomparable devotion of the hand that rocks the cradle, except the abiding love of God.

He conceived her love, therefore, whenever I am companionless and desire a listening ear, He is the attentive psychologist, as she would be.

Whenever I have need of a reassuring smile to silently applaud my conquest, God is standing in the arena clapping louder than all others, just like Mom.

Whenever I lack the sincerity of a sympathetic shoulder to ebb the flow of hot tears forming a watercourse down the canal of my flushed cheeks, He takes action as my lifeguard, spawning a channel of love where only one other being has awarded me a swim ... Mother.

A LADY

Someone who knows when to listen and when to speak
Someone who carries the persona of a lady at ease

Someone who attracts attention without saying a word
Someone who dares not mention the gossip she overheard

Someone who's comfortable in her skin
Someone who realizes beauty is not just about being thin

Someone who loves her neighbor as herself
Someone who asks if she can be of any help

Someone who smiles through a tear as if it weren't there
Someone who finds peace while kneeling in prayer

Someone who stands tall when all else falls
Someone who knows upon whom to call

PART 9

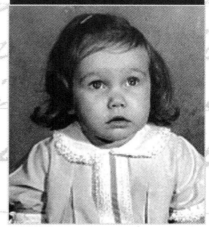

Chubby Cheeks

Father's Day

- Prayer Cries Help
- Prayer Cries Help (poem)
- Uniquely True
- It's Me
- Time Flies

Prayer Cries Help captioned my brain waves, painting a mental picture of innovative headlines intended for translation. Uncommon conclusions traced my steps as I attempted to construe the underlying meaning of the news bulletin transmitted to my intellect. Contemplating supernatural interpretation, I abstractly wandered over an experience of childhood, to catch a piece of action stolen from Bayou Country.

The city of Monroe, Louisiana, hosted a revival assembly featuring the evangelistic ministry of my Father, when a severe thunderstorm rocked the 29 foot travel trailer our family of four called home. As our close quarters violently seesawed back and forth, as if to collide head-on with an electrifying lightning bolt, Father steered us four and no more down the right track, leading to our rubber-wheeled automobile.

Bombarded by rain buckets of cats and dogs, my juvenescent ticker took strides to race like the wind, whistling heartfelt lyrics; rain, rain, go away, come again some other day. Frightened out of my wits, I kept watch as hardwood trees beat the bushes to the base drum of thunder, while cordless voltage lit the footpath to their head over heels nose-dive that excessively wiped the floor of earth.

As soon as the torrential downpour made a clear-cut decision to follow a trail exposing greener pastures, Father reclined his head to *rest his eyes*, as he would say. Quivering like a rabbit, I began to plead, "Daddy, please stay awake, you're my safe one." Privy to the butterflies fluttering inside the pit of my stomach, Father enveloped my fragility, giving confidence to security, even with his eyes closed. With a tower of strength acting as my pillow, I curled up closer to the man in the driver's seat, relaxing my six year old peepers, silencing the inner cloudburst with tranquility of trust.

Even as parental Father produced promised results of safety, so also does Heavenly Father speak peace of mind to a whirlwind of fleeting thoughts hurtling headlong in an effort to ransack the temple of the Holy Spirit. Leaving no stone unturned, He provokes my internal will to succumb to carpet-burned knees of flesh and cry, "Help!"

Even Asaph confessed, *"I cried out to God for help; I cried out to God to hear me,"* (Psalm 77:1 NIV). An anonymous author once testified, *"Then they cried unto the Lord in their trouble, and He delivered them out of their distresses,"* (Psalm 107:6 NIV). On the pretense of insanity, David wrote the psalm, *"The righteous cry out, and the Lord hears them,"* (Psalm 34:17 NIV).

On the eve of my triple-word eye-opener, *No Occupancy* labeled the threshold of my secret place. However, relying on literal decoding of the heading, *Prayer Cries Help*, enabled me to acquire abundant courage to make an about-face while lodging in the changing room of grace. Nowadays, *No Vacancy* is manifest above my closet of prayer, housing cries for help within earshot of Heavenly Father's dwelling place.

PRAYER CRIES HELP

As a little child, terrified
I'd reach for Daddy's hand

As a little girl, I knew for sure
That he would understand

My cry for help
The fear I felt

My Heavenly Father
Loves me even more

He'd recognize my heart felt cry
Though from a distant shore

As a mother builds a perfect nest
For expectancies to come

I know Father always knows what's best
For His daughter or His son

When they cry help
His heart just melts

He sees himself in you and I
The similarities

We're children that He can't deny
When praying fervently

Prayer cries help
It's ringing out loud and clear

Prayer cries help
Distinguished by the message that He hears

He hears my cry in the night
And softly answers me
To Father's ears I cry distinctively

UNIQUELY TRUE

A Father's love is like no other
Uniquely different from even Mother's

He knows just when to lend a hand
Or when to smile and say, "you can"

Strength is found with each new day
When next to Daddy at work or play

His touch is gentle, yet so strong
When hugged by him, you belong

Within the circle surrounding you
The love of Daddy

Uniquely true

IT'S ME

Dancing in your eyes
Captured by the light
I see me

Growing from your grace
Learning from mistakes
Reflections of the me I want to be

Father
It's me

Here I am again
Reaching for your hand

Father
It's me

Running to your side
Seeking your advice

This is your daughter
It's me

TIME FLIES
Sherri D. Dyson & Marble Holley Joiner

She was only sixteen
Her curfew was midnight
Went on a date
It was love at first sight

Half past two
She's having a ball
Then she looks up on the wall

Clock strikes three
She jumps up in shock
Hoping that it will eventually stop

Ain't it funny how time flies?

It was four in the morning
She slipped through the back door
Daddy was pacing
His mind was racing

Where have you been girl?
You'll see him no more
This behavior I can't ignore

Look at the time
Do you see what it says?
It's four o'clock
You should be in bed

Ain't it funny how time flies?

Time flies when you're having fun
Time flies, no work to be done
It's only when you're having fun that time flies

Tick-tock of the clock
When is it gonna stop?

Ain't it funny how time flies?

Banana Curls

Christmas

- Unwrap Your Gifts
- Let Us Not Forget

It's Christmas morning! The children have scarcely caught a wink of sleep. Wishfully visualizing battery-powered fire engines with blasting sirens, and Cabbage Patch dolls well-stocked with wearing apparel and edible food, Austin, 5 years of age, and 4 year-old Hayley count sheep until they finally doze off for a couple hours of shut-eye before sunrise.

As the star of day sneaks a peek over the horizon, drowsy siblings are roused by suspense of impending expectations. Secretly conversing over whether to let sleeping parents lie, they silently slip into the festive family room to rummage through gifts displaying their names, Austin and Hayley. Jumping for joy, they spot a number of exclusive boxes standing in line for exposure by tiny hands.

The assortment of presents assembled neatly beneath the twinkling Christmas tree will soon lie in disarray from the shake, rattle and roll maneuvers of childish curiosity. While Austin moves his individualized container from side to side, Hayley shakes the components of her personalized package.

Even so, contents concealed by ribbons and bows will only catch the eye of the beholder after holiday giftwrap is discarded. For Austin to witness red flashing lights of his electronic fire engine, and Hayley to suitably dress and nourish her Cabbage Patch doll, they must first unwrap their gifts!

You may be a mover and shaker like Austin and Hayley, but have you unveiled your gifts in their entirety? Have you employed the potential concealed by the soul of your shell, or do you put on the ritz with a contemporary bow of the here and now that attracts attention, giving no voice to endowment of talents? Do you publicly relinquish impressive wrapping paper and present bows to view, or preserve wraps for a day off with insecurity?

In days of youth, I remember shaking like an aspen when my father would call upon me during testimonial service to vocalize words of praise. Quiet as a church mouse, I would verbally stumble through a short-winded statement of salvation to silently slide deep into my seat of shyness thereafter. Subsequently, no backward bones appeared when I seized the moment to occupy my comfort zone as a songbird. One gift remained enclosed while the other became exposed.

As a young, married woman of twenty-six, I was scheduled by my husband to premiere as a keynote speaker for a pastor's conference, giving emphasis to pastors' wives. Despite the fact I grew up in a pastor's home, I had nothing short of no experience as a pastor's wife at that time. Needless to say, wifely submission was temporarily tainted the day I acquired knowledge of this engagement!

Articulating insecurities, I asked, "What am I going to teach these women they haven't already experienced?"

My inner voice spoke, "They're not going to listen to someone in her twenties."

"They should be teaching me!" I exclaimed.

Intimidating self-talk was evident as I peeled the initial strip of masking tape from my self-contained speechmaker. Going out on a limb, I painstakingly unfastened the shroud from my soul to cast a brief look at the gift once concealed, now revealed. A pack-rat by nature, I methodically stashed the wrap for fear of future failure.

Nabbing an audience comprised of my preaching machine husband (Psst...he's the one who got me into this mess), alongside my listening-ear mother, my unbiased viewpoint mother-in-law, and my self-constructive bathroom mirror, I sought to pursue the posture of a preacher. While all other congregational prospects cut a wide path for fear they would hear hightlights of points in progress, I tapped into a private pipeline dispersing Heavenly pointers.

Hushed whispers echoed amid corridors of my consciousness saying, "Break a leg," as I took the first step toward the pulpit of public speaking. **Witnessing a sea of eyes and ears sizing me up by my years, I took the stand to break barriers of age-old perception, that young women have no expository impartations, for lack of life's lessons.**

Shedding shyness, unfamiliarity clothed me with boldness of a lion. Fluently expounding upon the international language of love, my tongue became loose at both ends. Through the process of interpreting God's dictation, I sensed an awareness of His presence. The instant God stepped on the scene, faces encompassing all races rallied to the cause of love, embracing my new-found gift, the anointing to speak.

My exposition of gifts has equipped me to pave the way for individuals laying groundwork for their exhibition of talents. Ministering cross-country, I repeatedly come to grips with that unsuspecting someone playing tug-o-war with insecurity and self-confidence.

May I inquire, "Where are you in-between those two words?" Only you know the answer...or do you?

A word to the wise: "Unwrap your gifts!"

LET US NOT FORGET

Christmas is a time for giving
A time for loving, living and sharing

A time for celebrating those you love
And loving the unloved

A time for recognizing those in need
And responding by planting a seed

A time for children to giggle with glee
When discovering their gifts under the tree

A time for grown-ups to tell the story
Of baby Jesus in all His glory

A time for joy, a time for peace
A time for laughter, and shopping sprees

In all the hustle and bustle around
Let us not forget what it's all about

The King of kings, the Lord of lord's
Baby Jesus, Mary's boy

PART 11

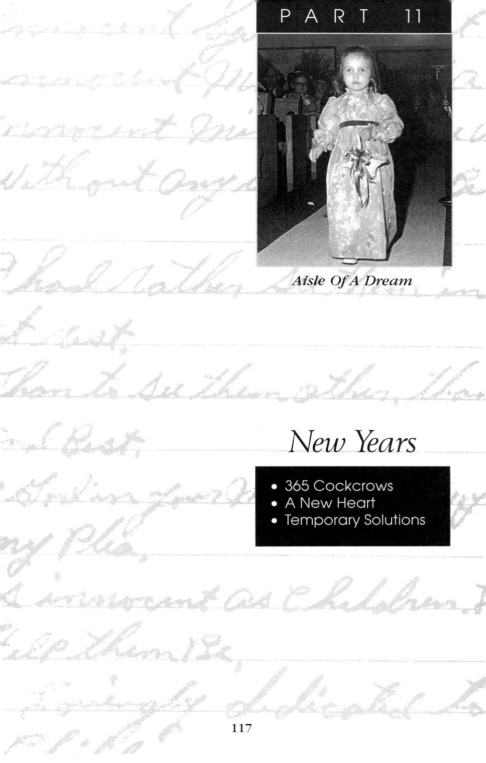

Aisle Of A Dream

New Years

- 365 Cockcrows
- A New Heart
- Temporary Solutions

117

Celebrating the expiration date of a preceding year with fireworks that spark enthusiasm for an uncharted period, ignites a plastered grin onto the cover page of free spirited personalities who have appealed for a revised lease on life. Throughout the preliminary 365 cockcrows, applicable candidates have groaned and rolled over as subjective lyrics, *Don't Worry Be Happy*, vibrate the radio alarm clock in chime with sunup.

In wake of pressing the 10 minute snooze button for the fifth and final time, they leap like a popcorn kernel from the land of Nod, and run like mad into the hustle and bustle of every Tom, Dick, and Harry, complimentary to claimants abreast of the times.

Petitioners penciling a jam-packed itinerary of presidential presentations, self-help seminars, mounds of paperwork in stiff competition with Mount Everest, 5 minute coffee breaks, and more meetings...will be granted one good moment to examine their lot in life. Will they see eye to eye with the conclusion of a predictable agenda, or eyeball the sum and substance of golden opportunity? Relative to the mind of man, is how a day begins.

New Years' resolutions prematurely give up the ghost more times than not, due to the misconception that a magical maneuver will materialize as a result of the grand finale, 12:01 A.M., January 1st. At its peak, the trick of the trade generally corresponds with the stereotypical punch line of a practical joke. In plain sight of April daisies, supermarket fat transfigures to lumpy cellulite of the hips, savoring yesterday's large curd cottage cheese as a matter of course.

A newborn year gives entrance to vitality by lingering beneath the inflow of daytide. The crack of dawn delivers a bill of exchange bearing the John Hancock of fresh expectancy; *This is the day the Lord has made; let us rejoice and be glad in it* (Psalm 118:24 NIV).

Individuals one stroke shy of red-letter enthusiasm may result in breach of contract. However, when the face of time points its forefinger at 11:59 P.M., and Cinderella loses her petite glass slipper for fear of being served as pumpkin pie, a direct rollover option is targeted for automatic renewal, postmarked next day air.

Awaking the dawn of sunrise, early light once again casts a brief look through the peephole of the horizon, to peer into the bay window overlooking daybreak's to do list clamped abreast the kitchen fridge with magnetic force. What role will optimism play in the scribbled text of what comes next?

With new years' festivities in full swing, resolutions are the thing. Why not opt to emphasize new *days'* proclamations, hot off the press of morning dew beginnings? Your answer will influence your tomorrow.

A NEW HEART

Smiles are evaded
Laughter is gone
Promises broken
By love that's gone wrong

Happiness left you
With sadness alone
But heartache paraded
Performing this song

A new heart, a new start
Is formed within His hands

A new heart, a new start
Is where your sadness ends

Begin new paths today
Believing in the Name

Giving you a new heart
A new start
Found in God's embrace

Look up for direction
The pathway's in place
Engulfed by compassion
Displayed by His grace

Where peace is your partner
And love is your friend
Streaming with laughter
That flows from within

A new heart

TEMPORARY SOLUTIONS

New Year's resolutions
Bring temporary solutions
To life's complications
And daily temptations

But who would have thought
That you would be caught
Eating a pie
In the month of July?

Never say never
But only believe
That you will be faithful
'Cause faith is the key

And when you are tempted
To eat when it's late
Remember your vow
To nibble and weigh

AFTERTHOUGHTS

The end of this book signifies the beginning of another. I remain on a perpetual writing binge, infiltrated with bittersweet tales of life.

As I depart this exit ramp, and step aboard a nonstop train bound for future moments, I will ceaselessly keep at my fingertips revelations of my God; the supreme storyteller of all time. He governed my source of council for *Can't Stop Love*, and brought to being its cover inscription by loving me completely.

Mission impossible became mission possible the hour I acknowledged the appointment of God's unstoppable love. Split-second decisiveness turned the tide of living water toward the bottom of my heart, dispersing an inflow of adoration provided by my Father.

Drenched to the depths, walls of bygones crumbled at my feet, exposing my nakedness before God, injecting showers of blessings into my spiritually dehydrated soul. Vulnerability bathed me with affection, while clothing me with Godly love.

My God is no respector of persons. He extends immortal love to His creation, and offers tender passion toward human nature, unconcealed and accessible to those special made by divine design.

From your stance and location, do you visualize the love of God as earned wages for good behavior, or an inheritance for one and all? God's love is a gift bestowed, no strings attached. His heart's desire will make you whole, no questions asked.

Lonely heart, look to Jesus, His love will never leave you wondering why.

Exploring worldly pleasures
Has left you empty handed
A vacancy is opened in your heart

An occupant is waiting
To fill the void within you
And gracefully accept you as you are

CAPTION QUOTES

"When it comes to accomplishing your dream of fiction, leave no stone unturned to substantiate a figment of imagination into a fact of life."

"Recurrent storylines instruct me to weather the storm and celebrate the rainbow."

"Life's season finale will be determined by how well I follow directions."

"True love is far more than impassioned conceptions, but rather, a lifetime commitment to another person or being."

"Mature lovers invoke qualities within their partner, and seek clues to discover attributes underlying shortcomings of their better half."

"Freedom from guilt allows us to turn around and face the mirror, exercising mature love by sifting through our own imperfections with a fine-tooth comb."

"Memories legislate a family possession, which designate future generations to glimmer from the past, assuming far more than monumental superstructures or bank accounts."

"Expect to be cheerful, and transfer happiness in the process of your joy."

"S. T. O. P. – See The Overall Picture."

"The slip and fall of topsy turvy days periodically suggest I shut up shop and take stock of God's unique idea: me."

"Has a round stone replaced your song?"

"Scripts aren't always written with explanations. Although postscripts sometimes follow."

"Opinions should be readily available instead of ready made."

"Regard your indiscretions as wisdom acquired, and your fumbles as safeguard in the face of a tackle."

"Whenever I have need of a reassuring smile to silently applaud my conquest, God is standing in the arena clapping louder than all others, just like Mom."

"Relative to the mind of man, is how a day begins."

"A newborn year gives entrance to vitality, by lingering beneath the inflow of daytide."

"What role will optimism play in the scribbled text of what comes next?"

"The end of this book signifies the beginning of another."

"I remain on a perpetual writing binge infiltrated with bittersweet tales of life."

"From your stance and location, do you visualize the love of God as earned wages for good behavior, or an inheritance for one and all?"

IN BLACK AND WHITE

Photography - Courtesy of SDD Publications

PART 2, page 27; *Triking By Trees*, Sherri D. Dyson, 1972

PART 3, page 33; *Kiss Of Destiny,* Timothy J. and Sherri D. Dyson, 1994

PART 4, page 41; *Far Away Look By The Brook*, Sherri D. Dyson, 1976

PART 5, page 47; *Baptized At Four*, Sherri D. Dyson and Rev. Denver L. Stanford, Sr., 1973

PART 6, page 69; *Pregnant With Preston*, Sherri D. Dyson, 2000; page 74, *Bundle Of Blue*, Preston Kendall Dyson, 2000

PART 8, page 89; *Say Cheese*, Sherri D. Dyson, 1970

PART 9, page 101; *Chubby Cheeks*, Sherri D. Dyson, 1971

PART 10, page 111; *Banana Curls*, Sherri D. Dyson, 1974

PART 11, page 117; *Aisle Of A Dream*, Sherri D. Dyson, 1973

Photography - Courtesy of Michelle Stinek Studios

PART 1, page 13; *Together In The Heart,* Timothy J. and Sherri D. Dyson, 1998

PART 7, page 81; *Black Tail Affair*, Sherri D. Dyson and Dominoe, 1998

Penmenship - Courtesy of SDD Publications

PART 1 - PART 11, pages 13, 27, 33, 41, 47, 69, 81, 89, 101, 111, and 117; *Innocence*, original penmenship, the late Rev. T. P. Johnson

Graphic Prints - Courtesy of SDD Publications

PART 6, pages 75 and 76; *Special Delivery*, original handprint and footprint, Preston Kendall Dyson, 2000